Flogging The Czar

FLOGGING THE CZAR

poems by

Robert Winner

The Sheep Meadow Press
New York City

ACKNOWLEDGEMENTS

Abraxas: "Your Name." *American Poetry Review:* "The Ruler," "Death," "The Chain Gang." *Confrontation:* "Life Insurance," "Into My Dream." *Croton Review:* "Night Landing." *Cumberland Poetry Review:* "Clayton," "Morning at White Pond," "The Table," "Part of an Argument," "Two Photographs." *Helen Review:* "Flogging the Czar." *Ironwood:* "A Fire That Suddenly Wakens," "At Congo Tires," "Machines." *A Just God:* "In the Hospital," "The White Birch." *Kavitha:* "An Anniversary Gift," "Jazz Recording Session." *Negative Capability:* "A Cargo of Parrots," "Shakespeare." *New Letters:* "South African Gold Miner," "Miss Alderman." *Ohio Review:* "Shark." *Poetry Now:* "Dawn," "The Instrument." *Response:* "Diaspora." *Slow Loris Reader:* "Driving in a Storm," "Evening," "February Morning Through My Kitchen Window."

The poem "The Banjo" appeared originally in *The New Yorker*.

Published by The Sheep Meadow Press
Distributed by Persea Books,
225 Lafayette Street
New York, N.Y. 10012

Library of Congress Cataloging in Publication Data

Winner, Robert, 1930-
  Flogging the Czar.

  I. Title
PS3573.I5323F5   1983   811'.54   83-603
ISBN 0-935296-38-7
ISBN 0-935296-39-5 (pbk.)

Manufactured in the United States of America
First Printing

For my Mother
and for the memory of
my Father

Contents

III

IV

"What is the price of Experience? do men buy it for a song?
Or wisdom for a dance in the street? No, it is bought with the price
Of all that a man hath, his house, his wife, his children.
Wisdom is sold in the desolate market where none come to buy,
And in the wither'd field where the farmer plows for bread in vain."

Blake: from The Four Zoas

I

Machines

Most beautiful when they're turned off,
with scales of dirt on them, with our lives
all over them — derricks
hanging over the Passaic River
at rest in the smoke-dimmed sun
like rust colored washerwomen . . .
the light clean airplanes parked at Teterboro
aimed at a speck of sky to disappear in . . .
the white-decked grain ships at Welland Canal
rising or falling in the locks . . .

They make me realize something beautiful about *us*
we're going to die for. I want to forget
missiles sweating in their silos,
the poisons near Niagara, the scream of mills.
I think of men in the backwoods
of Putnam County — how crushed and lined they are
after only a few years —
how they love rifles, outboard engines,
can openers, old pickup trucks . . .
extensions of us, carnal and beautiful
things we'll die for.

The Ruler

Measured at school, lined up
against the gymnasium wall, or before that
the power of dimes and marbles—or later:
locker room comparisons, ball scores,
test grades—and finally: checkbooks,
taxes, horsepower, serial numbers, etc.

How did all these accountants
crash the party of the glands,
and build their second skeleton inside me?
I want to disorganize my life.
I want my days unmeasurable.

Maybe the careful weighing at my birth,
the morning I learned to tell time
from a clock in a Chinese laundry,
counted cracks in the pavement, or felt
the ruler's pressure on my head—
like the flat of the sword on a knight's
shoulder—were signifying moments,
saying to me as all of me listened,
"This is what is most important about you:
your length on earth, your shadow
a measurable thing."

A Photograph of My Grandmother at Nineteen

She is taken in the glow of mahogany
and silver, in the embrace of oak,
her lace dress buttoned to the chin,
her brown hair falling straight...

It pleases me she was once desirable,
not what I knew — a mat of wrinkles,
scraggled hair, thin-lipped
pillowings in a cancer hospital
...shrunken Grandma — soft speech,
bones and whiteness.

Ignorant, I took that ghost for her,
I gave her no right to be young,
ripe for marriage with some well-to-do bachelor,
a match for any of them with her brains
and childbearing body.

For the first time, I'm sorry for her,
seeing her young, all promise...
no poverty yet, no daughter
killing herself, no husband
dead three decades.

She goes on living in the vast amnesia
of trees, stones, wildflowers,
in my own fears, in humility and stubborn
fists and Bronx sidewalks and bits of grass
that remember no one,
in the dining room clamor of the family,
the table never large enough.

The Automat

Machines began to do the eating,
with bigger mouths.
Once, it was like eating in the subway;
yet something was magical in those huge rooms
—chrome, bright acres of tile and marble,
three-decker sandwiches on thick white plates,
food coming out of the walls

in little windows opened by nickels,
a dream of the future
when no one would have to do anything
but drink hot chocolate or roam in cars
around an electric countryside.
Machines would serve mankind
with almost human pleasure.

They're all gone now, Automats,
and the illusions of the 1939 World's Fair.

A Sepia Photograph of My Grandfather

He's sitting on cushions in the middle of Asia
wearing a turban, a hookah near him
and a scimitar.
        From Lodz, a textile merchant,
he travelled like a Phoenician,
buying cotton in Bokhara, Galveston, or Egypt.

It seems miraculous how they went everywhere
like English milords—those Jews
walking the thinnest silver line
of toleration.
        To escape the pogroms,
he sold his factory and his house
and slipped across the border with his family—
from Poland to Germany, my mother
hidden in a clothes trunk—
and then to England, where his business failed,
at last America—penniless,
used up, his name changed.

Here, in this faded card, still young,
he's playing out the charade of his adventure—
that short half-century of freedom
between ghetto and holocaust.
As if he knew it would end in human smoke
he took, reluctantly, that wandering step
to find another country, another street
where they could put their bundles down,
light candles, bake their bread
and spread the cloth for their festivals.

Diaspora

1
Even the grass should know our legends,
green in spring outside
the lion-colored walls, the rooted houses
down on their knees with age.

We never leave that old land
beating the sun back with its rock-
strewn hillsides, its sheep,
its dust of secrets...

Others can live and die like leaves,
can lie down easy as grass and sleep,
while the Jew
tosses on boards or silk, and remembers
tall thin ghetto houses, food stalls
lining a sewer, mongrel villages
waiting for Cossacks.

2
We are in love with being ourselves,
a people whom death seeks out and can never finish,
a neck of suffering that never bends enough to die.

And shame. There is that canyon of shame
on streets where they beat you.
Anyone else has a country of blood and numbers,
a confidence you can never earn from banks
and stately houses, or learn from sacred books,
but have to pluck from the dreams
of your steel-eyed ghetto fathers,

gnawing your nourishment from the bones
of all their survivals.

And of course they're right, the goyim;
there is no homeland, there is only
skin, bones, muscles, entrails —
everyone alike.

That's why I go on whispering in exile.
        Shema Yisroel.

Part of an Argument

Oh I get it
sun, cafes, fruit stands, newspapers . . .
you don't want Jews to be wall-clinging mourners anymore.
You want us all to be microwave technicians,
plant geneticists, Sanskrit professors . . .
two dimensional and staunch as recruiting posters.

. . . Bathing suits, oranges, traffic, public relations experts
that won't let us have our weird, bent,
weeping and muttering grandparents in the house,
or the ones who didn't know how to survive
the outcry for victims, and their visions
of doom's black clothes in the closets,
their dark like raisins,
and the sour twilight of ghetto shops.

Let me have my lament, my darkness,
my cry so wonderful it has made tears break
from murderers' eyes . . .

Listen to me,
landscape architects, dockworkers, surfers, hotel developers . . .
you want me to be straight-backed and proud as my young
      grandfather
stepping down in 1890 on a free land.
I can't forget his freezing prayers before dawn,
his lies, his phony diseases, his game
doomed leaps at appearances and the big time;
a dandified success American driving his Ford,
and Vandyked Litvak Talmudist in his prayer shawl.
He was a wilderness to his sons . . .

A mystery,
our fervent temples clinging to the world.

My Hunchbacked Uncle

If you were art, we'd find you
howling with Breughel's beggars,
black zeroes for eyes and mouth,
but you were not blind, you saw them also.

Your blue eyes asked me:
"Why do I share their bed straw
and their stone pillows?
Where is the genius of my body hidden,
calling to me from under stone?"

Inconsolable,
you swallowed Marx, Freud, chemistry, languages.
Too late.
It was always too late for the body
inside you, the child
with bare legs kicking through air
from a swing in a green Polish yard.

The Bicycle

The bicycle disconsolate for decades
among used lumber in the garage rafters
lies embedded in its year—fifteen—
which I can never let go, which is
no litter of the past, but myself
on the rim of the horizon
when the walls of my father's house fell open
and I was outside, everywhere on my own.

Two Photographs

The family picnic in 1937:
my boy face grins into the sunlit Kodak,
with relatives forty years older or dead
looking pleasant forever
into my eyes —

and that other photograph in *Life*
of the Loyalist soldier
shot dead, falling sideways in Spain
his rifle mid-air at his knees
and the flag of his hair left blowing
where it had been.

Those details: the lifted hand,
the hair, the folding knees . . .
Even homesickness seems caught
in his falling.

How many times his life has been saved,
and mine, and my relatives
eating fruit on the lawn
that summer day. Our faces in a snapshot
call up the gallant in themselves
like dumb animals enduring only
the present. I try to hold

everything in that present,
because every day the impossible
seems more necessary, every day
idealism pulls at me — wanting too much
like that soldier —
one of my many defenders

14

one of my own lives
                    unhelmeted
with no insignia on his makeshift uniform,
his cartridge belt and his hair outlasting him,
the canteen floating at the former level
of his ribs, and his hand still lifted.

Flogging the Czar

"We have no army. We have a horde of slaves cowed by
discipline, ordered about by thieves and slave traders..."
—L. Tolstoy: *A Plan For The Reform of the Army (1855)*

I want to flog the Czar!
I want him dragged out of his silk
to make him feel the fear-flushed chill
of one who is led to flogging.

I want to paint on his soft back twenty centuries
of screams, the odors of pus and gangrene,
the death-smell of ashes buying
with the worthless currency of ashes
wheat fields and apple trees.

I want to celebrate the day
the people didn't forgive him,
returned the bullets to their guns,
the guns to their crucibles,
the crucibles to their clay,
the clay to its sleep.

II

February Morning Through
My Kitchen Window

What can it tell me?—this raw,
unornamented back of an apartment house,
an inward face
with grime streaks struggling down.

And what can it tell me?—these rows
of bathroom windows like the dripping of faucets,
slow lights behind blind slats
of bedrooms assenting to morning,

And the complications of the rooftops,
planes and angles irreducible as bone—
what can it tell me?

They tell me death is plentiful
and everywhere, that all there is
is wall, table, gas-flame, bread...
things and their stubborn purposes.

Clayton

A ghost walks over the tracks
at Harmon's railroad yards
in slate-blue work clothes,
pale arms bloodless as steam,
a negative of coal they burned here
forty years ago.

If Clayton haunted anywhere it would be
this grimed brick locomotive shed —
twenty years of his sweat in concrete floors
and bright red handkerchiefs —
he would inhabit its vacancy like a bird call.

He lived above our garage in the 1930's
waiting out the Depression, paying rent
with handyman's work.
I remember the smell of his kitchen,
the oilclothed table, tin plates,
coffee, hand-rolled cigarettes.

Railroads were the line of escape,
the knot-hole across a continent.
Boxcars rolled through his one-track home town,
making shelves uneasy, shaking the widow's cups...
The ink-blot engine, elephant slow,
lumbering out of a wall of leaves;
the engineer on his throne, the brakeman
walking backward on the tops of cars,
wheels that could sever a body, the bruised
steel plates and damaged colors of
boxcars; Burlington, Lehigh, Wabash...
Clayton's mythology.

His blue eyes sharpened with flame
when those huge wheels rolled away from him.
"Power", they kept repeating, "Power",
taking his breath and blood and lifting them
into the glamour of the horizon.

I think of his blue-veined arms, brick red in summer.
I think of his intelligent, defeated eyes
I think of how he edged towards freedom,
wanting to be used like a nail, to give his body
to the engines of a giant company
bankrupt now.

Driving in a Storm

Rain stammers on the steel roof.
Wind, unable to touch us, mauls the trees.
We push through miles of its slaver

past trees which build only themselves
past drenched fields—cows and horses
trying to shrink their bodies
under dripping leaves.

What have I built with *my* hands
that can almost smile like wet steel
into the eyes of lightning,
or roll untrembling, bearing down
—thunder on thunder?

I live in shelters built
by the enormous hands of grandfathers
and great grandfathers; their backaches,
tired eyes, brains that wanted
to cut rock, purl through timber.

All their victories bought me
this steel shell tunnelling through rain.
But hard as they worked, the storms
worked harder: thunder building itself,
rain pouring into rain, rain drowning,
wind eating its own tail, cars'
water-disheveled windshields crazed
by oncoming headlights, bearing down.

Wall Street

Getting money, not poems
from these spit-thin streets

Searching out the grains for bread
among these cornices
these pigeon roosts
this stone of money dark Manhattan

The poem never leaves me out of itself

The poem recites me from sidewalks and windows
from cracks of sunlight over a city
foreign to me as Asia

Its voice calls down to me from glazed hand-lettered doors
the half-truths of my ambitions...
the years go forward on my hungers
like a narration.

Getting my bread
just that
eating it, fleshing out, decaying

Bread must be the poem that always exists
my body's meaning
moving me through hallways
past marble where spring hides
past rivers locked in wood

The secretive insistent meaning
of the elevators the clocks
the faces of clerks

the cop retired to his bank job
the desk the telephone
the white shirt
the window's question
"Why not get out of here?"
the numbers crawling across the walls
the poem

Getting my bread, the poem
can never deny me
its voice.

Morning at White Pond

The silence circles from my oars,
touching the shoreline's mass of hemlock
— boughs dipping to water.

I cast my long lines out
to pull the silence from water,
retrieve from wilderness
morning in back of the mania,

remembering ages of lull before my birth,
before ambition drilled
into my skull, and my name
and all its possessions were pounded in,
and my trail cut out of this green
unmotivated wilderness.

Life Insurance

The salesman comes at me—
expensive suit, a leopard's eyes,
soft-footed mastery of hunting.

And I delight in this
and like to run with him,
and step in opposing circles,
seeking the throat.

He doesn't want only money from me,
but a little more life to his days,
another day in which to feel
the power to overcome someone...

Not hungry, but afraid of boredom
—a life without events—
his paunch sags, his legs
grow heavier, and he smells
the small gray lizard of death...

We shake hands, neither of us
truly essential to the other's life—
having lost nothing from this
bloodless combat.

The Banjo

There is some demon turning me into an old man,
living like a tapeworm in my gut,
turning me into a snowman
of cleaned up fingernails and shaving cream,
while somewhere in the life I forgot to live
an old rapscallion banjo sleeps with dust.

I'd like to take that banjo to my job
and sit cross-legged, strum and strum
and wake those rigid people into dancing —
those white men so white their smiles are water,
those camouflaged men who cruise
around each other like soft battleships.

I'd like them to remember their bare feet,
the bite of dust and sun down country roads,
the face they forgot to desire
carved and wrinkled as a peach pit...

All of them nailed to their careers
like handles on boxes!
There is some other game for me,
another reality could walk in any time
and become the boss,
shouting Dance! Dance! Dance!
Dance through partitions!
Dance through stairwells, envelopes, telephones!

It's hard to know which life is sleep
or where the door is with my real name on it.

South African Gold Miner

(Witwattersrand, 1950)

His life abstract to me as the word
eternity, I'd have to extinguish
the fury in my eyes, deny the trees,
remove myself — like an animal —
from history's fabrications, forget the sun
and the bird that sings in the baobab tree...

I'd have to go down
into the nexus of the mine,
cage-lowered a mile below grass,
antelope, women, sky — the Transvaal Plain...

I'd have to work next to his sweat
to understand the ruins of his eyes,
their eloquence like coffins or dead stars...

I'd bring him out in one lunge
to plains-grass, women, sky, antelope,
and cover him with bracelets and rings
of gold, ancestral gold, and white plumes
torn from the bird that preens itself
over his landscape, singing.

Into My Dream

My mother limps home bleeding.
Like everyone, even the poor,
she had too much on her to be safe.
Somewhere a mugger ransacked her purse,
threw out keys and photographs,
kept the cash.

I've seen the slums — the trouble:
they've got too much on *us.*
It's no use raging.
Everything we lose is payment.
Their mothers also have bodies.

That night two black men walk into my dream
and sit on my lawn
and lean their elbows on my grass
and nothing I say moves them
or gets them out of there.

Segregated Railway Diner — 1946

I sat down in the colored section
in my sixteen-year-old's gesture.
He sat facing me in his life.

A thin smile licked his lips
and disappeared in the corners. Outside,
gray unpainted cabins, red clay yards
where black men and their calico women
watched the slick trains pass —

It buried me, that smile. It said
I didn't know enough to sit with him
in that lacerated corner.

He studied his plate when the captain came over,
M.P. face the color of butcher's meat —
rapping me on the shoulder with a heavy pencil,
arm grip steering me to my assigned seat.

The Chain Gang

Stripped to the waist,
hard-muscled, downcast, under the guns
of lounging guards, they are clearing a roadside
across a palmetto landscape.

I notice one blond boy swinging a pick,
broad-shouldered. His skin is smooth, bright, sweaty.
His upright body ripples
under the rigid fury of his face.

His bulging eyes fixed on the ground
can see mountains, the destiny
of his imagination he can never get to,
where he could rest, a lion
in the wilderness of his flesh.

I see the body with its own career of gestures—
its bright roads, its dark roads
apart, serene...

Men must be carved, apparently,
like slaughtered steers or pigs
to find the marble of their bones
innocent,
innocent after all
as the stones they break, or rain,
or the guards in cages of their white voices.

Trapped in one chained line,
one terrifying combination of arrangements,
driven to taste each other's flesh...

31

The body sings alone
among the earth's arrangements
ignorant of crimes or dreams
or the curious idea of justice.

Night Landing

Descent is over the sea,
a black mirror of black sky,
a dark grasp of nothing,
the coastline amber with electricity—
America burns all night.

Road lights, ganglia
of towns and shopping centers—
from the air tiny
outposts of desire:
the need to have comfort
of night lights, the need to have:
cars and intersections.

I know I'm gliding down
from light too intense,
like understanding darkness—
seeing the sea's black star
describe the word *alone*,
the land's small fires
spell *hunger*.

Shark

He pulls his jaws together,
tears and swallows. It makes no difference.

His mouth like a black moon,
he slaughters his way through the sea,
his mouth his only soul, his genius.
It makes no difference.

He must carry his need around,
he must cure his hunger,
he must trail his emptiness through the bloated water.

Who can find enough meat?

Who can float this bubble of want?

Who can fill this sea-bowelled mill of guts?
It makes no difference.

The sea is eating itself through him.
The sea keeps swallowing its fish through the bowels
                                        of other fish.
The sea withdraws his life like a card from a deck.
It makes no difference.

III

Mozart

Anytime we want, he'll sing for us
an aria from *The Magic Flute*.
He walks up all our dark stairways
carrying his candle.

Bug-eyed, bewigged Mozart
inwardly gazing, inwardly singing to lift us
clear of sadness and disillusionment.
God, how the keys miss Mozart!

To be human was to be like a god!
He'd have carved his love songs
on the bark of trees. He'd have sung
without ink or keyboard.

On his deathbed, Mozart begged to hear
Papageno's bird-catcher's song.
He wanted the Clown to sing.
Even Mozart needed Mozart then.

At Congo Tires

The garage is filled with the clangor of wheelrims,
the curses of men bent over tires,
their crushed nails, grease-smeared overalls
and hands, their boots enclosing
a thousand miles of painful arches and caked sweat.
Dirt here has entered their skins forever
from roads like a ghostly network of flayed rubber.

I need my fingers up to the knuckles in dirt.
I need the bulging neck of the manager
bellowing through car windows.
I need the power of the machine that clasps
the tires with an easy spin on rims.

It will let me know how to lie on grass,
to understand the thousand faces of grass
straining away from my weight,
to grasp the one idea of life there—
to simply exist—green dynamite
in the solitude of green,
as if it were enough
to be real as things are.

The Instrument

I've seen the mahogany grow pale
under the huge shoulders of pianists,
the curved beams brace themselves.

Such an army, so many games of chess
on the infinity of the keyboard, so much
access and self-disclosure...

It's like climbing in a forest
formed by your own hands, or singing
with your armpits, groin and heels...
it's playing Mozart in the Amazon
to a naked wondering people.

Music—the world that might be,
and yet the world as it is. The heart
comes out of hiding, saying to us:
"Listen, you can say anything you want now.
Here is the instrument."

Learning to Mourn

I'm an inexperienced mourner
I don't even know how to begin
to cry out like that old man
wailing in the next hospital room —
oi weih, oi weih — his two sounds
beating against the wall.

He makes me squirm
but I get his message better than my own.
How can I free myself like him?
How can I know my place as he does,
know how little I am?
How can I mourn, the cheep of a trapped bird
crying out violent sorrow?

Old man, teach me.
Help me reach the bowels of my cry
and bring it up, coarse, rasping.
Teach me to be disgusting.
Help me to exile myself from all
the populations of eyes and ears.
Teach me to live in that country
where no one else is, where I can
bash to pieces my good breeding,
my priests and pillars
— no illusions, the *self* wiped out,
unable to see or hear or understand.

Old man — lying in your shit —
you've let the angel of death from your mouth.
One minute of your unforgiving protest
is like true song: reckless, fatal singing,

song that is not victorious, not even consoling,
merely a sound you have to make.

Phenomenal Men and Women

My eighty-year-old arthritic mother
angled like a used nail,
pushing her garden wheelbarrow...
my wife who would take my suffering
out of my soiled eyes into her own
clear green ones...my friend
in the South who saved my life,
dying now of Parkinson's disease,
who could repair the broken
bodies of coal miners...

My father said to me once
with sorrow that stunned me
"I'm a mediocre man."
I've argued with him silently
long past his death, having seen him
"rising to the occasion"
like the ascending saints with their toes
still pointing earthwards —
phenomenal how they rise
how we all rise.

Jazz Recording Session

A zoohouse of windbag birds, blowhards
suckling their strength in the warmup
—solo fragments, breaks, riffs...
each man kept to himself, drank coffee
from paper cups, cracked private jokes.

Given the beat for the quick
first number they came together
in one voice, a blast of concord—
nails, teeth, hair, skin, nerves, muscles,
straining to reach the throat of the melody
to touch

its concealed life
the final statement for everyone,
(as I listened in the control room,
hardly believing
there were streets outside like broken pianos)
as I heard
their brass alive shining brotherhood.

Evening

My mother sleeps in her chair.
Her magazine lies face down on the floor.
With her body, she tells me
everything that's happened to her—
her face is like torn-up earth,
her mouth hangs open, stuck
in the middle of a frightened question.

What can I answer—
the lies we tell when we're awake?
The play is over, it's tucked away
in the empty pockets of furniture
and silver boxes given by aunts.
Now, a bare stage stares under a light-bulb,
stripped to a matter of facts, agnostic
of passion or footsteps or names.

The Last Gift

An old man struggles up the aisle
of the dark theatre,
trying to get out fast.
With pain he moves one foot
in front of the other.

His wife follows close
behind him, saying over and over
"I'm going with you."

On the screen, a man
passionately kisses a woman;
her tongue explores his mouth.
The old man topples from step
to step, his wife's clinging
plagues him until he yells out
"Christ, leave me alone!"

It covers her like poison.
He is enraged by pain.
He can't stand dying alone.
He wants her burnt with him
on his funeral pyre.

My wife also tells me
"I'm going with you."

It will take all my strength
to free her at the end,
to stop her falling into the flame
already searching my body,
to keep its poison from spreading

over her, or its tongues
from gorging on her.

An Anniversary Gift

I want to give you flame, comfort
and total comprehension, the discovery
and capture of fire, our lives
in tapestry complex as the Bayeux,
or Bach.

That would be it, or closer to it.
That would be one sentence telling it all.
That would be a scarf you could wear
all year, all years.

You know my shoulder, its strength,
I want to make it into a token
like a Persian miniature —
a compressed world of flowers and blood,
passion, painstaking care
and unexpected wings.

Summer Solstice

Epithelial as snow-crust, the daylight
clings last to flakes of white clapboard
and grass in the open meadow.

Another year wanders off,
another year I haven't believed enough
in each day's sacred step

climbed slowly, an Aztec priest in black robes
taking a heart in my hands
that might be my own...

I've worshipped sun all my life.
It slinks away. I'll hunt it
in the winter intimacy of fire—

the light that is always young, the burning
that goes as far as it can within us,
shares everything with us
but the end of things.

Death

It is silent as a garden spider.
It hangs there, waiting patiently.
It has eaten everything and never grown bigger,
still the size of a thumbnail.
I know that I am the fat one.
Everything that has lived is on my side
—the quickness of birds and snakes,
the glowing eyes of horses at night,
even the voracious sea-slugs that eat
the still alive flesh of drowning bodies.
All of the dead are alive in me,
are ranged within me like an army.
They sing against you, little arachnid star,
against you, immobile hanging gut.

IV

Miss Alderman

By the high steel hospital bed
a thousand miles from anyone I knew,
she sat while I slept:
Miss Alderman, night duty student nurse
with auburn hair, blue eyes, a perfect body.

Sixteen, just inside girl hunger,
paralyzed, sleeping on my side,
I dreamt of her in my fever,
my spine like a broken chair
on one of their broken Southern porches.

Coming out of sick half-sleep, I found her
pressing my face with her parted lips.
Desire leaped in me, all my body
helpless to respond like a sack of gravel.
I could see her breast.
A warm deep wave of her carried me off.
She kissed me, fondled me; she cared enough
to want to give me
some of that which haunts me,
heals me, makes things right.

It haunts me now that only chance with her,
that tenderness
lost to me in some provincial Southern city,
a nurse still maybe, or a housewife.

I knew it was no more
than kindness
by the blank calm way
she fixed her hair at the mirror

and scraped her lipstick
with her fingernail
and buttoned her dress
afterwards.

In the Hospital

The sun can die like anyone,
splintered among shadows.
A clatter of purposes rises from the street.
Cries float up like corks.

Pain is bright,
and the heart, how easily it vanishes
in foam on the lips.

I dream of a dawn rising without birds,
a white sun striding over blind streets,
the shadows thick and dark.

I move among them, tracing
their indifferent forms, like clouds
with the accident of life.

A Cargo of Parrots

With words torn out of the mute
bloody-tongued—
"heartsick", "suffer",
no longer casual syllables but groans
of their oldest meanings—

all others' grief seems light
—a full sailed sloop hauls off
the whole world's misery
like a cargo of parrots...

All those wings and noises!
Why can't that fat ship take to the air?
They say this being alone with pain
is common, living through it
while the world billows around you...
Tears are the language, tears
that cut me free like acetylene.

Paralyzed

Who am I to expect
immunity, not to feel
blows from the ceiling and walls,
flame-throwers at the window,
or sorrow's commonplaces?

Rows of books in my shelves
move away at dusk like a convoy
humming outbound, hopeful.
I need to join them,
to take an indeterminate journey,
to grasp the earth like rain,
to exist in the trees if I have to.

Not an easy thing
to break myself into enough pieces
to cling to everything,
or to think about the idea of God,
or the bodies of women.
No easy thing, "back to the wall,"
not to become stone.

Shakespeare

When I was bound by sickness to a ceiling, walls,
a scrap of deaf-mute sky in a window-frame—
you gave me back the earth;

when they were ten floors under my window
you helped me smell the rainy streets again
and feel the textures of steel and cloth and waves,
and hear the voices of men and women
speaking their guts out...

Even more than music you rescued me.
Your people packed my room like a marketplace:
Falstaff, words delicious to him as wine
or capon, mocked the clanking nobles,
Hotspur mounted a stallion of words,
Macbeth was dragged by words to lunacy,
Bolingbroke, dying of words in council,
finally spoke his need for his son's love.

I am in love with their voices—
no one too low for eloquence, too high for misery—
telling me all the news of England or Italy,
the loot of living, the inexhaustible
plenty that saves all of us.

Killing an Ant

I crushed an ant on my desk
and watched its six legs
tearing the air like oars
of a whaleboat hurled out of water...

I saw my own body straining
to escape death, to live forever.
I pressed my thumb once more
to the ant's black carapaced body;
its mandibles reached for my hand,
an almost brotherly gesture.

The Table

This table of polished wood
with slender currents running through it,
with its poise that stands in another corner of feeling
from my dreams and griefs,

upholds so much,
this wooden tortoise shell, this ox,
between bowls of soup and coffee
sleep and trees, upholds

the lines of this poem which seek
the quiet discourse from the bottom of things
in these close-linked, long-fibered tongues.

A Fire That Suddenly Wakens

I lay on concrete
in the burned out barn.
I felt the ruins
of sea-life that had died
and become limestone.
I felt the cold
marrow-silent depth of the sea,
deeper than the reach of words.
How it denied me.
How it threw the sun back into the sky.
How it looked down and down only.
How it centered on darkness:
the end of its travelling
back into stone.

It refuted happiness: the climb
through sunlit fields; the piano sonatas
taking strength from my fingers;
the smoothness of hair; the hypnotism
of water. The floor was all stone entrails
writhing towards a shape that still eluded it.
I felt the sand grains through my shirt,
ground up, slung, sifted into submission.
I lay there, a body that had lost everything
but the weight of bones.

The sky looked in, a laughter
that began on the first serious day,
the birthday of anything that had to die.

I knew I would rise from the ground
at last, hardened by its refusal to let me enter.

Like a tree my fate still leaped in the air.
Like a kangaroo, like gravity
demanding another body, like an oar that—
pulled by water—pulls against it,
like a fire that suddenly wakens
after midnight, when the fire is out,
a lion with a red mouth leaping through
the crumbled body of a log,
the hollow fingertip of night,
the burned out center, bone cold.

The Invitation

It's wonderful—the blonde
comes out of the restaurant
and smiles. Could angels manage it?
—this dazzling come-on, this fire
splashed out of nowhere like the sun
on that fourth Creation day—
what a smile that was!

The Dance

This rooted sinuousness,
this slow arousing of the oak
and blacksnake, the attack of leaves,
leaves opening pink mouths:
it is the carnival of oaks and snakeblood,
earth's carnival, clod's *kermess*.

You want to go up in flames, coiling
the other body like a vine or serpent.

Deadly? The dance leans upward,
the earth pulls downward,
birth so close to death
they almost touch.

Your Name

I want my metaphor for you
life-sized, not diminutive —
not like grandfather's *kätzchen*
or my father's *chickadee*
for women who could crack
apples open with their hands.

Of course, the men tried to make them forget
the mops and galvanized washboards,
the stir and kneading of enormous meals,
and the humility of walking one step behind.
They wanted to recover the play of love.
"Rough winds do shake the darling buds of May."
They did.

My metaphor for you won't be a bird
or kitten, but an experience —
the soft late light of early summer,
every tree full of easygoing leaves,
and every species alive, abundant,
and we not worrying about darkness
or getting home.

Dawn

You lie on my bed at daybreak.
Your pale skin draws the faintest
light to itself like water.

How many dawns I waited!—
in childhood sleep, the years I lay awake
at war with my body—

to see you rise from my sleep all fresh,
like snow fallen overnight on dead grass
nailing my testament of sadness to a tree
for the wind to finish.

The White Birch

The white birch
storm-bent over the ground
like a torture victim—
for years an upright sliver
in our summer back yard—
drags down wires, will have to be
sawed up, stacked on the woodpile.

Deep in its grain
one straightest line of light
persists, one shining that was itself,
as yesterday its leaves were
eyes of the spirit.

About the author

Robert Winner was born in The Bronx in 1930. He graduated from Sarah Lawrence College in 1952 and became a stockbroker in 1956. In 1976 he retired as vice president of a leading securities firm to become president of the Lakewood, N.J. Cemetery Association.

Robert Winner's poems have appeared in numerous periodicals, including *The New Yorker, TransAtlantic Review,* and *Ohio Review.* His first book, *Green in the Body,* was published by Slow Loris Press in 1979; a chapbook, *Origins,* was published by Slow Loris Press in 1980.

Other poetry titles from The Sheep Meadow Press:

Peter Balakian
Father Fisheye
Sad Days of Light

Chana Bloch
Secrets of the Tribe

Hayden Carruth
Brothers, I Loved You All

Edward Field
A Full Heart
Stars in My Eyes

Arthur Gregor
Embodiment and Other Poems

David Ignatow
The Notebooks of David Ignatow

David Jones
The Roman Quarry

Cleopatra Mathis
Aerial View of Louisiana
The Bottom Land

F.T. Prince
Collected Poems
The Yuan Chen Variations

Dahlia Ravikovitch
A Dress of Fire

Alberto Rios
Whispering to Fool the Wind